mighty machines

MOTORBIKES

Written by
Chris Oxlade

Illustrated by
Peter Gregory

p

This is a Parragon Book
First published in 2001

Parragon
Queen Street House
4 Queen Street
Bath BA1 1HE, UK

Produced by

David West ♀♂ Children's Books
7 Princeton Court
55 Felsham Road
Putney
London SW15 1AZ

British Library Cataloguing-in-Publication Data

A catalogue record for this book is available from
the British Library.

ISBN 0-75254-673-2

Printed in U.A.E

Designers
David West
Aarti Parmar
Illustrators
Peter Gregory
(SGA)
Mike Lacey
(SGA)
Cartoonist
Peter Wilks
(SGA)
Editor
James Pickering
Consultant
Steve Parker

CONTENTS

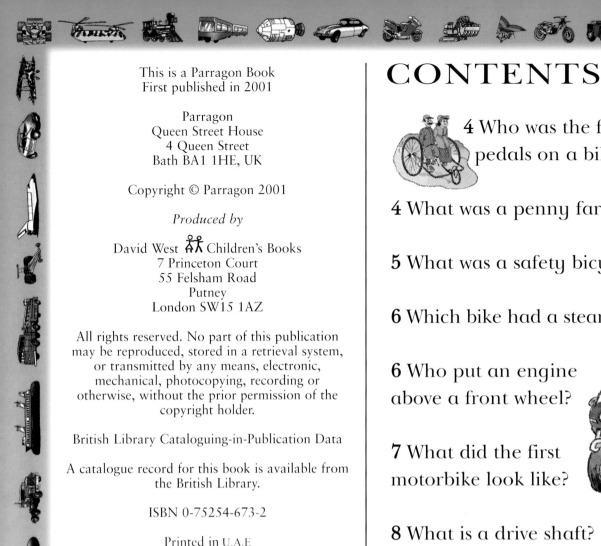

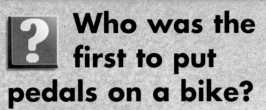

❓ Who was the first to put pedals on a bike?

In 1838, a Scottish blacksmith called Kirkpatrick Macmillan built the first bicycle with pedals. Before this, bicycle riders kicked the ground to move along.

Kirkpatrick Macmillan

4

Penny farthing

❓ What was a penny farthing?

A penny farthing was a bicycle of the 1870s, named after two British coins. It had an enormous front wheel (the penny) and a small rear wheel (the farthing).

Amazing! In the 1880s, couples often rode side by side on tricycles (cycles with three wheels) called sociables. Each person had a set of pedals, which turned the huge rear wheels.

? What was a safety bicycle?

The safety bicycle was the first bicycle to look like today's bikes. It appeared in 1885. It had two wheels the same size, a diamond-shaped metal frame, pedals that turned the rear wheel using a chain, and brakes worked by levers on the handlebars.

Is it true?
People raced tricycles.

Yes. In the 1880s, the tricycle was not just a cycle for children, as it is today. It was popular with adults too. Tricycle racing was one of the first forms of cycle racing. Race events were held on bumpy roads and wooden tracks.

Safety bicycle

Which bike had a steam engine?

The Michaux-Perreaux bicycle of 1869 had a steam engine under its saddle. Wood or coal had to be put in the engine every few minutes to keep the water boiling, to work the engine.

Michaux-Perreaux 1869

Who put an engine above a front wheel?

The Werner brothers in France built a motorcycle in 1899. It was a safety bicycle with a petrol engine above the front wheel, in front of the handlebars.

6

Werner 1899

Amazing!
American engineer Lucius Copeland made a motorcycle by adding a small steam engine to a penny farthing. He rode the bicycle backwards, using the small wheel to steer. The machine could travel at 20 kph.

? What did the first motorbike look like?

The first proper motorbike had a heavy wooden frame, wooden wheels with metal rims, and two stabilising wheels to stop it toppling over. It was the first motorbike to have a lightweight petrol engine, but it was very slow. It was built by German engineers Daimler and Maybach in 1885.

Daimler/Maybach
1885

Is it true?
Early motorcycles had pedals.

Yes. The engines on early motorcycles were not very powerful or reliable. So the bikes had pedals for going up hills or in case of a breakdown. Some modern bikes, such as mopeds, still have pedals.

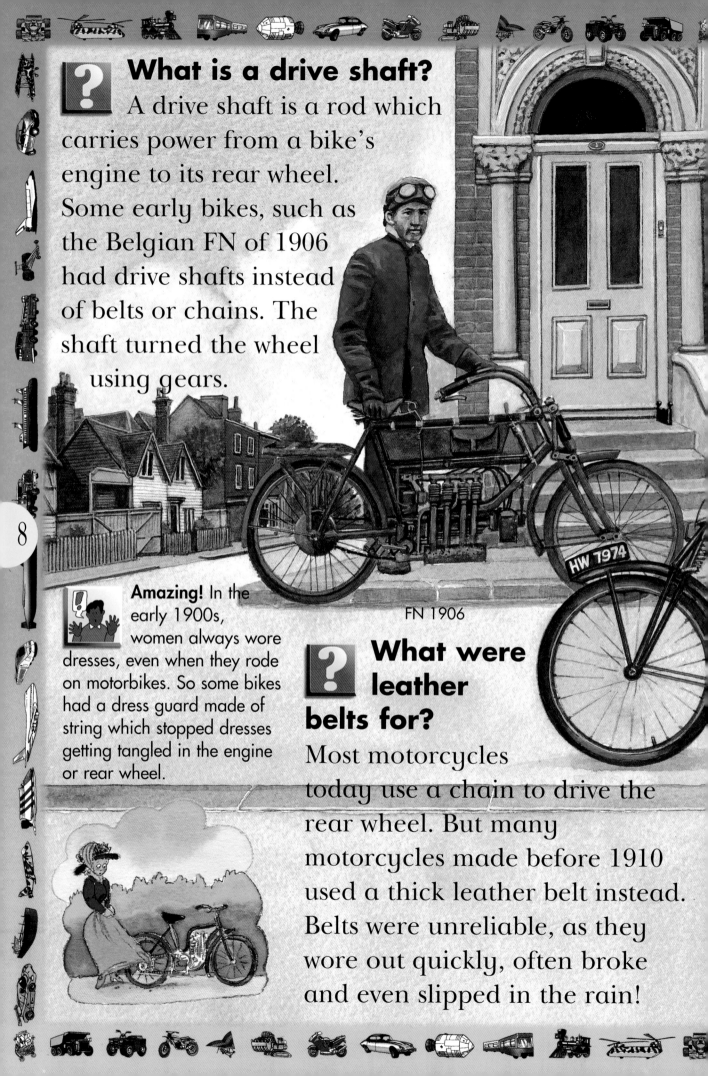

? What is a drive shaft?

A drive shaft is a rod which carries power from a bike's engine to its rear wheel. Some early bikes, such as the Belgian FN of 1906 had drive shafts instead of belts or chains. The shaft turned the wheel using gears.

FN 1906

Amazing! In the early 1900s, women always wore dresses, even when they rode on motorbikes. So some bikes had a dress guard made of string which stopped dresses getting tangled in the engine or rear wheel.

? What were leather belts for?

Most motorcycles today use a chain to drive the rear wheel. But many motorcycles made before 1910 used a thick leather belt instead. Belts were unreliable, as they wore out quickly, often broke and even slipped in the rain!

❓ When was a drive chain first used?

Most modern bikes have a flexible metal chain which carries power from the engine to the rear wheel. Chain drives were introduced on some bikes in the early 1900s, such as the 1905 Scott. Chains are made up of dozens of short pieces linked together.

Two-stroke Scott 1905

Douglas 1911

Is it true?

Belt drives are still used today.

Yes. Most modern bikes use a chain drive, but some have belts instead. The belts are made from rubber, strengthened with fabric. Belts are lighter than chains and need less maintenance. A few modern bikes have drive shafts instead of a chain or belt.

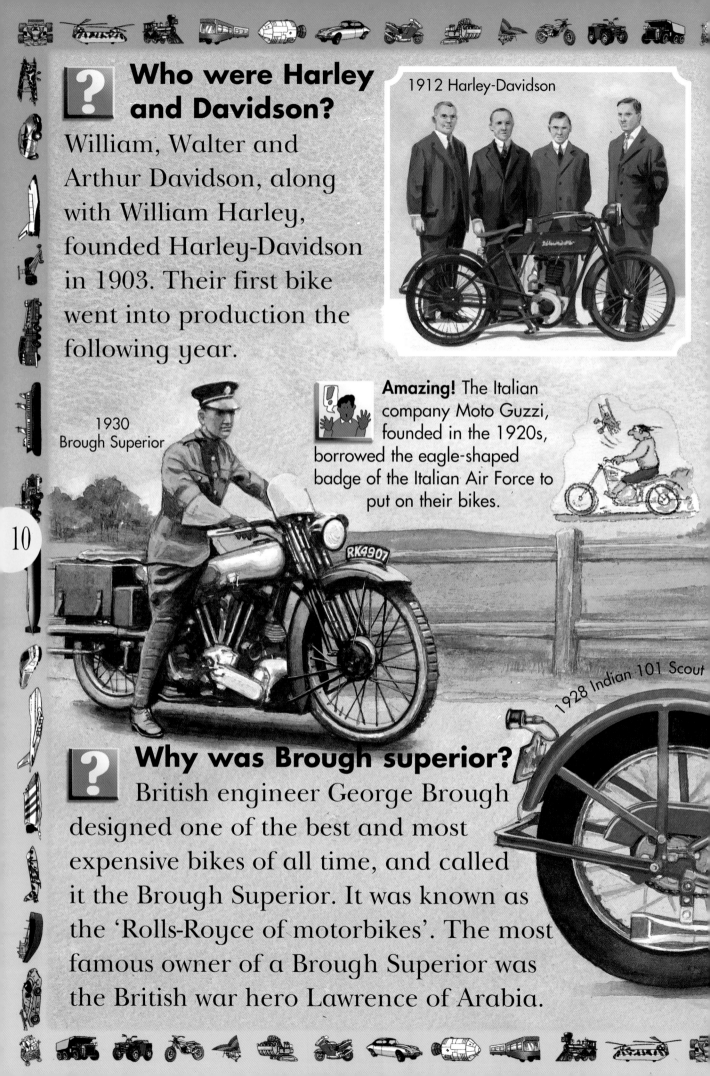

? Who were Harley and Davidson?

William, Walter and Arthur Davidson, along with William Harley, founded Harley-Davidson in 1903. Their first bike went into production the following year.

1912 Harley-Davidson

1930 Brough Superior

Amazing! The Italian company Moto Guzzi, founded in the 1920s, borrowed the eagle-shaped badge of the Italian Air Force to put on their bikes.

1928 Indian 101 Scout

10

? Why was Brough superior?

British engineer George Brough designed one of the best and most expensive bikes of all time, and called it the Brough Superior. It was known as the 'Rolls-Royce of motorbikes'. The most famous owner of a Brough Superior was the British war hero Lawrence of Arabia.

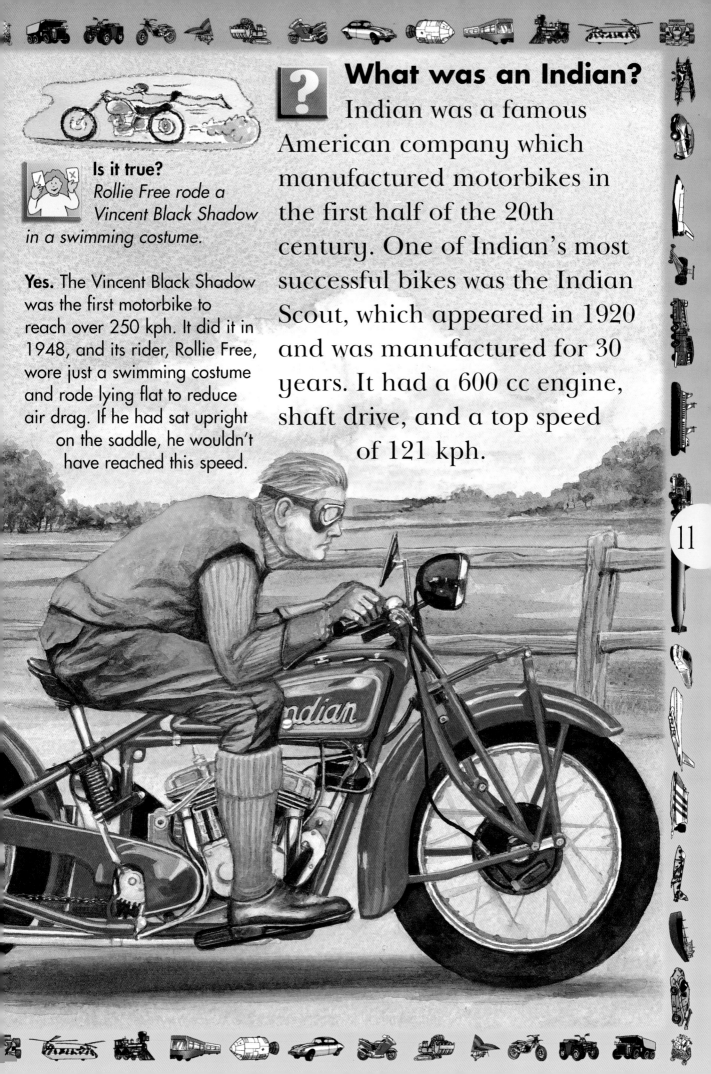

Is it true?

Rollie Free rode a Vincent Black Shadow in a swimming costume.

Yes. The Vincent Black Shadow was the first motorbike to reach over 250 kph. It did it in 1948, and its rider, Rollie Free, wore just a swimming costume and rode lying flat to reduce air drag. If he had sat upright on the saddle, he wouldn't have reached this speed.

? What was an Indian?

Indian was a famous American company which manufactured motorbikes in the first half of the 20th century. One of Indian's most successful bikes was the Indian Scout, which appeared in 1920 and was manufactured for 30 years. It had a 600 cc engine, shaft drive, and a top speed of 121 kph.

? Where is a motorbike's engine located?

A motorbike's engine is between the two wheels, attached to the bike's frame. Above the engine, just in front of the driver's seat, is the fuel tank. Exhaust pipes carry waste gases from the engine to the rear of the bike.

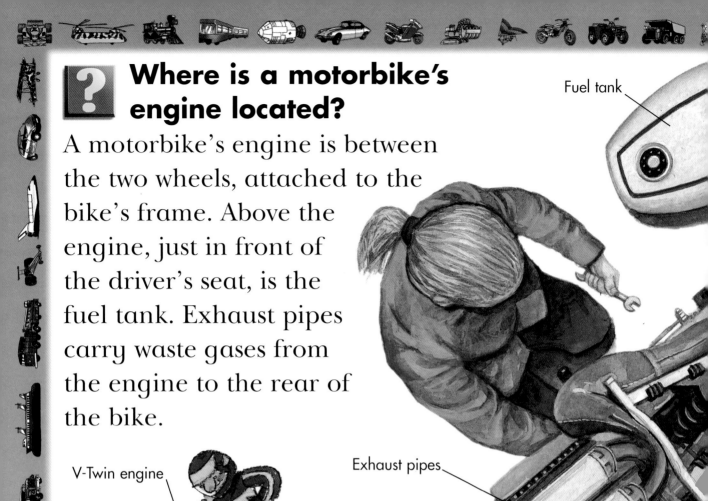

Fuel tank

Exhaust pipes

Cylinder head

V-Twin engine

12

? Are motorbike engines all the same shape?

The shape of an engine depends on how many cylinders it has and how they are arranged. A v-twin engine has two cylinders in a V shape. A straight-four has four cylinders in a line.

Amazing! The biggest engine on a motorbike is a 1600 cc engine on a Yamaha superbike. The engine is as big and powerful as the engine in a family car.

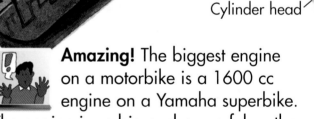

Yamaha 1600cc

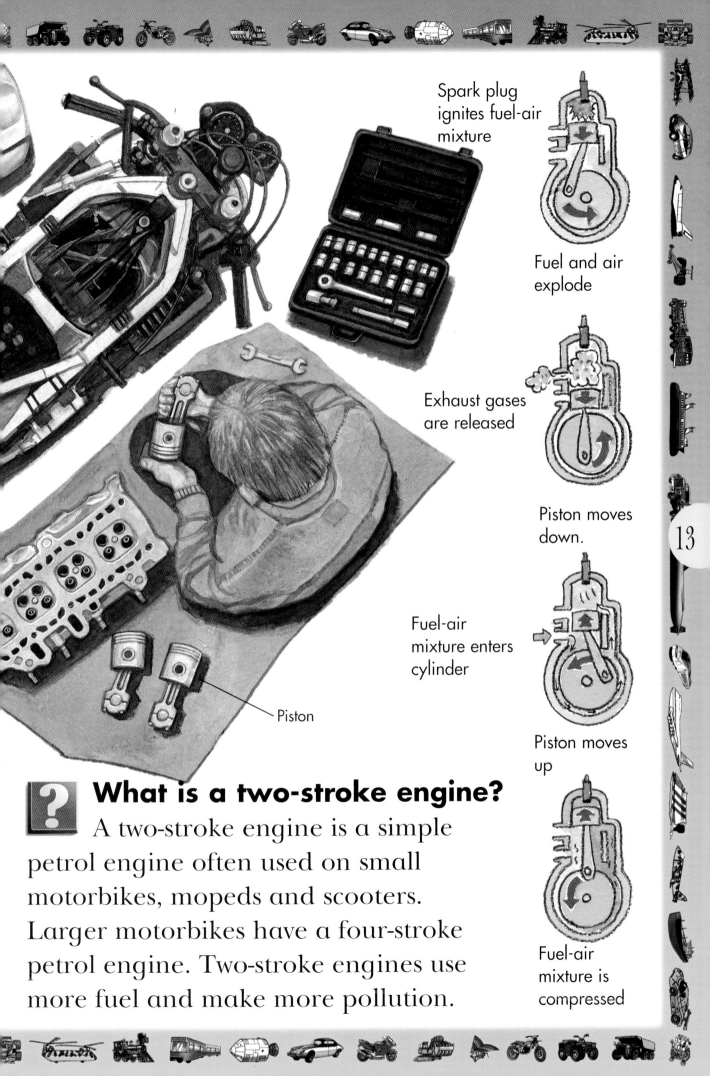

Spark plug ignites fuel-air mixture

Fuel and air explode

Exhaust gases are released

Piston moves down.

Fuel-air mixture enters cylinder

Piston

Piston moves up

13

? What is a two-stroke engine?

A two-stroke engine is a simple petrol engine often used on small motorbikes, mopeds and scooters. Larger motorbikes have a four-stroke petrol engine. Two-stroke engines use more fuel and make more pollution.

Fuel-air mixture is compressed

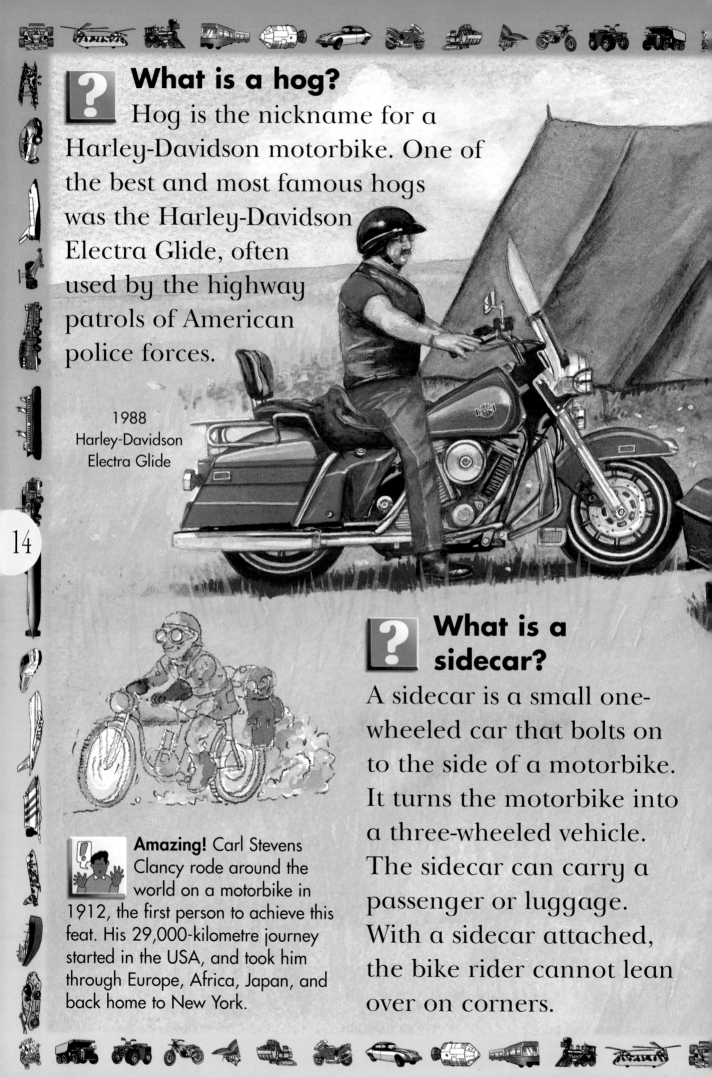

What is a hog?

Hog is the nickname for a Harley-Davidson motorbike. One of the best and most famous hogs was the Harley-Davidson Electra Glide, often used by the highway patrols of American police forces.

1988
Harley-Davidson
Electra Glide

Amazing! Carl Stevens Clancy rode around the world on a motorbike in 1912, the first person to achieve this feat. His 29,000-kilometre journey started in the USA, and took him through Europe, Africa, Japan, and back home to New York.

What is a sidecar?

A sidecar is a small one-wheeled car that bolts on to the side of a motorbike. It turns the motorbike into a three-wheeled vehicle. The sidecar can carry a passenger or luggage. With a sidecar attached, the bike rider cannot lean over on corners.

? What is a Gold Wing?

A Gold Wing is a giant touring bike made by the Japanese company Honda. The Gold Wing is very smooth to ride, has a seat for a passenger, and an engine powerful enough to pull a sidecar and a trailer. It's perfect for long-distance touring.

1982 Honda Gold Wing with sidecar and trailer

15

Is it true?
Passengers used to ride in baskets.

Yes. The bodies of sidecars for early motorbikes were made of wicker, which was also used to make baskets. Wicker is made by weaving bendy wooden branches together.

? What is a scooter?

A scooter has small wheels, a small engine near the rear wheel, and a gap in the frame for the rider's legs. They are cheap to run and good for nipping around busy towns and cities.

16

Amazing!
You can buy toy motorbikes which are models of real bikes, with tiny engines and the same controls as a full-sized bike. They're not allowed on the road though.

Italjet Millennium 125

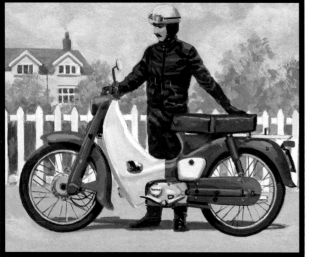

? Which is the best-selling motorbike ever?

The 50 cc Honda Super Cub, which went on sale in 1958, is the biggest selling motorbike ever. This little bike is cheap to run, and is still popular all over the world.

Is it true?
The scooter is a recent invention.

No. Scooters became popular in Italy in the 1950s, and in the 1960s they became very trendy. They were ridden by young British men called mods, who dressed in green parka coats and customised their scooters with lots of mirrors and flags.

Yamaha YP 250
Majesty

Which scooter fits in a car boot?

The American-made Autoped, which was produced in 1915, could be folded up to fit into the boot of a car. In recent years, as traffic has become busier, fold-up scooters have become popular again for cheap and speedy travel.

21st century scooter

 Amazing! Trials bikes can make short hops up almost vertical rock faces. The rider needs good balance and expert control of the clutch and gears.

❓ What is a trials bike?

Trials bikes are designed for riding on steep, rough and rocky ground. They are ridden in motorbike trials, where riders have to ride over obstacles without stopping or putting their feet down to balance.

Trials bike

❓ Which bikes have knobbly tyres?

Trials bikes and motocross bikes have tyres with a deep, knobbly tread around the outside. The tread helps the tyres to grip the wet and muddy ground during competitions.

Motocross

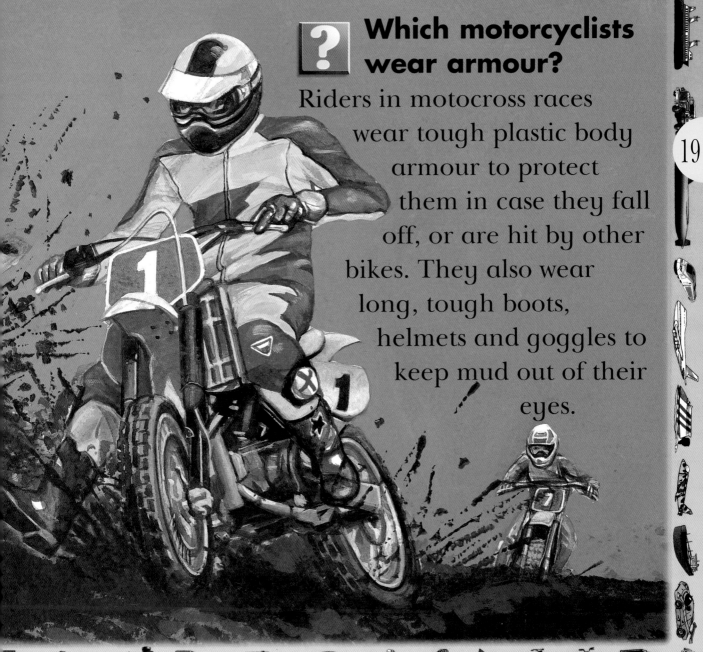

Is it true?
No one has crossed the desert on a motorbike.

No. Riders often take part in motocross competitions held in deserts. There are also long-distance desert motorbike rallies, such as the Paris-Dakar rally which crosses the dusty Sahara Desert.

Paris-Dakar rally

Which motorcyclists wear armour?

Riders in motocross races wear tough plastic body armour to protect them in case they fall off, or are hit by other bikes. They also wear long, tough boots, helmets and goggles to keep mud out of their eyes.

1942 Harley-Davidson WLA

? Who had a holster on a Harley?

US Army despatch riders of World War Two carried a rifle in a holster on their Harley-Davidson WLA 45 motorbikes. More than 80,000 WLAs were made during the war, and many of them were bought by ex-soldiers afterwards.

20

Is it true?
The first US soldier to enter Germany after the First World War rode a Harley.

Yes. Corporal Holtz, an American soldier, was photographed riding into Germany on a Harley with sidecar, the day after the war ended in 1918.

? Who dropped from the sky with mini bikes?

During World War Two, when some Allied and German soldiers jumped from their aircraft, their mini motorbikes parachuted down with them.

German mini-scooter

? Who had machine guns on their motorbikes?

German World War Two soldiers rode high-speed BMW motorcycles with sidecars. One soldier operated the heavy machine gun in the sidecar.

Amazing! In World War Two the German army used a vehicle called a Ketten Kraftrad that was half motorbike, half armoured car. It had a motorbike front wheel and caterpillar tracks.

21

BMW R-75

? What is a TT race?

TT races are held every year on the public roads of the Isle of Man, part of the British Isles. TT stands for Tourist Trophy because, when the races started in 1907, they were for touring motorbikes.

Norton Isle of Man TT racer

1915 Harley-Davidson

Is it true?
All motorbikes have brakes.

No. Motorbikes built for speedway racing have no brakes, and only one gear. These races take place on oval tracks made of dirt, sand, grass, and sometimes ice. The riders slide round the bends at each end of the track.

? Who raced on wooden boards?

Early motorcycle races used to take place on wooden bicycle tracks. Imagine the splinters if you fell off!

What is a superbike?

A superbike, such as this Ducati, is a very fast motorbike, normally with an engine of 750 cc or bigger. The word 'superbike' was first used to describe the Honda CB750 of the late 1960s. Superbikes are designed for high-speed racing but can also be used for touring on public roads.

Amazing! In high-speed crashes, motorbike racers sometimes skid across the ground at 250 kph! So racers wear leather overalls to protect them in case they fall off. They also have tough knee pads sewn into their leathers because their knees touch the road as they lean into bends.

Ducati superbike

Modified Triumph Thunderbird

Amazing! Chopper motorbikes and tricycle motorbikes are popular with motorbike gangs called Hell's Angels. Hell's Angels wear all black — black leathers and black helmets.

What is a chopper?

A chopper is a customised bike with a low seat, high handlebars and long front forks. The rider leans back, as if in an armchair. Choppers first appeared in the USA when Harley owners chopped up parts of bikes to make much lighter and faster versions.

Chopper

? Who reached 345 kph on a Triumph?

Johnny Allen rode a cigar-shaped Triumph bike at 345 kph across the Bonneville Salt Flats in America in 1956. Triumph named their most famous bike the Bonneville after this feat.

Is it true?
Chopped scooters are used for drag racing.

Yes. A drag race is a race between two motorbikes along a short, straight track. Some drag racers compete on chopped scooters, which are scooters with a beefed up engine and a long frame.

? Who put three engines on a motorbike?

Russ Collins put three engines on to his Honda drag racer in the 1970s. Drag bikes need a huge amount of power for maximum acceleration, and some models are even powered by rocket engines!

Russ Collins

? How do you go faster on a motorbike?

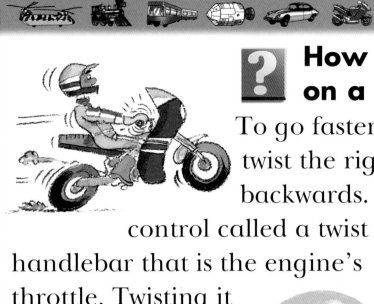

To go faster on a motorbike, you twist the right-hand handlebar backwards. There is a control called a twist grip on the handlebar that is the engine's throttle. Twisting it backwards sends more fuel to the engine, making it turn faster and speed up the bike.

? How do you slow down?

To slow down quickly on a motorbike you pull the brake lever on the right handlebar and press the brake pedal with your right foot. The lever works the front brake and the pedal works the rear brake.

Clutch lever

Throttle

Front brake lever

Rear brake lever

26

? How do you change gear?

To change gear on a motorbike, you pull in the clutch lever with your left hand, change gear with your left foot and let out the clutch lever. Pressing up and down on the gear-change foot lever changes the gear.

Is it true?
Motorcyclists kick start their machines.

Yes. Most motorbikes have an electric motor to start the engine, but they also have a kick-start mechanism in case the starter breaks down. All early bikes had a kick-start mechanism to turn the engine.

Gear lever

27

? Why do motorcyclists lean over on corners?

Motorcyclists lean their motorbikes over as they go round corners to stop their bikes toppling over sideways. The further they lean over, the faster they can go round the corner.

? Which racing bike has no front forks?

The Honda Elf Endurance racer was the first racing motorbike without front forks. Instead of forks, the bike had lever arms to support the front wheel. It raced in the 1980s at Le Mans.

Is it true?
Some motorbikes had steering wheels.

Yes. The bizarre Militaire motorbike of 1912 had a steering wheel instead of handlebars. Balancing was difficult, so the bike needed stabilisers.

Honda Elf

elfe 9

elfe

elf
HONDA

DUNLOP

Amazing! The smallest motorbikes are very tiny indeed! The world's smallest is ten centimetres long, with wheels two centimetres across. It has an engine and can be ridden (but only just!)

28

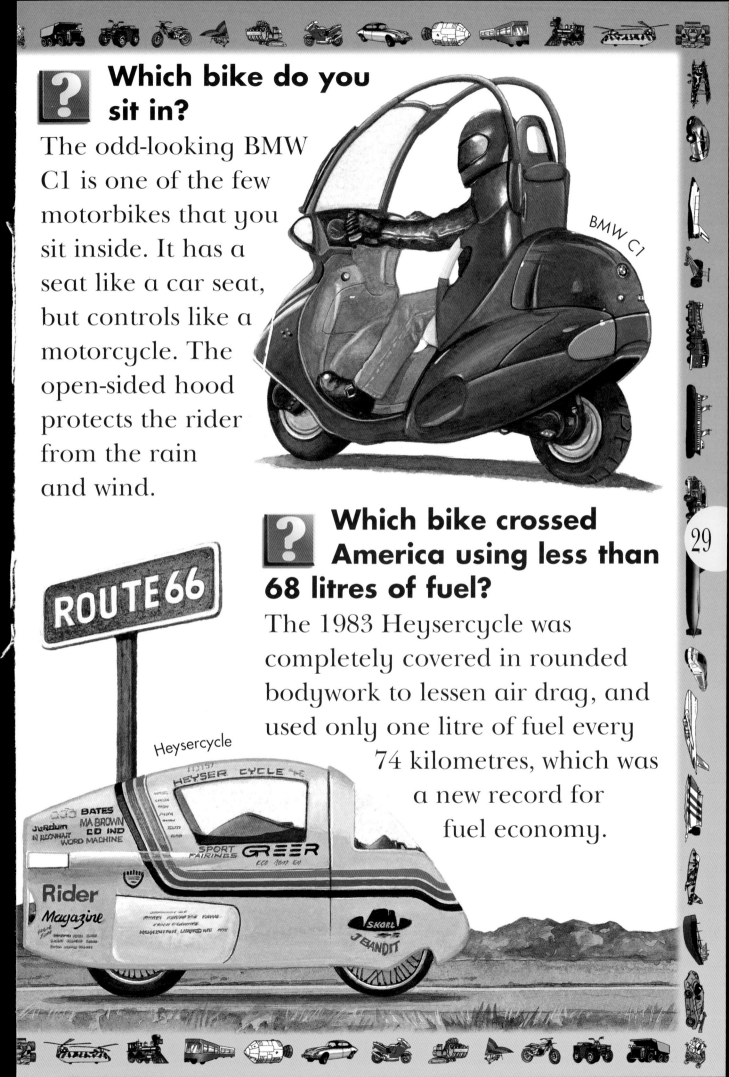

? Which bike do you sit in?

The odd-looking BMW C1 is one of the few motorbikes that you sit inside. It has a seat like a car seat, but controls like a motorcycle. The open-sided hood protects the rider from the rain and wind.

BMW C1

ROUTE 66

Heysercycle

? Which bike crossed America using less than 68 litres of fuel?

The 1983 Heysercycle was completely covered in rounded bodywork to lessen air drag, and used only one litre of fuel every 74 kilometres, which was a new record for fuel economy.

? What is stunt riding?

Stunt riders speed up ramps on their bikes, and jump over cars, buses and trucks. The most famous stunt rider of all, Evel Knievel, even tried to jump a canyon in a rocket-powered 'skycycle' in 1974. He nearly drowned in the attempt. Evel claims that he has broken every bone in his body!

Evel Knievel

Amazing! Teams of stunt riders perform incredible tricks such as building motorcycle pyramids and jumping through rings of fire. For a pyramid, the team members balance on each other's shoulders while the bikes are moving.

Wall of death

? What is the wall of death?

The wall of death is a circular, vertical wall. Stunt riders whizz round and round it on their motorbikes, as if they're riding inside a tin can! They have to ride at full speed to stop falling off the wall.

❓ What is freestyle motocross?

Freestyle motocross is a new motorbike sport where the riders perform daring tricks as they jump off humps on a dirt track. Sometimes they even let go of their bikes completely!

Is it true?
Riding on one wheel is impossible.

No. Riders can lift their front wheels off the ground and ride along on the rear wheel. This trick is called a wheelie. Superbike racers do wheelies to celebrate winning a race.

Freestyle motocross

Glossary

Brakes Devices that slow a bicycle or motorbike. They work by pressing pads firmly against the spinning wheels.

Clutch A device on a vehicle, which controls whether or not the power from an engine reaches the wheels.

Cylinder A chamber inside an engine inside which pistons move up and down.

Drag A force caused by air flowing around a moving object which slows it down.

Drive shaft A rod that links an engine with the wheels of a vehicle. The engine turns the rod, which turns the wheels.

Pedal A plate that a rider presses on with his or her feet to make a bicycle or moped move along.

Petrol engine An engine in which the pistons are pushed out by a mixture of petrol and air exploding.

Sidecar A single-wheeled car with a seat that attaches to the side of a motorbike.

Stabilisers Small extra wheels on each side of a bicycle or motorbike that stop it toppling over sideways.

Steam engine An engine in which the pistons are pushed in and out by high-pressure steam from a boiler.

Tread The pattern of grooves around the outside of a tyre.

Tricycle A bicycle or motorbike with three wheels, normally one at the front and two at the rear.

Index